WHEN JUSTICE FAILED

THE FRED KOREMATSU STORY

BY STEVEN A. CHIN

ALEX HALEY, GENERAL EDITOR

ILLUSTRATIONS BY DAVID TAMURA

RSVP

RAINTREE
STECK-VAUGHN
P U B L I S H E R S
The Steck-Vaughn Company

Austin, Texas

Published by Steck-Vaughn Company.

Cover art by David Tamura

Printed in the United States of America
2 3 4 5 6 7 8 9 R 98 97 96 95 94

Library of Congress Cataloging-in-Publication Data

Chin, Steven A., 1959–
    When justice failed: the Fred Korematsu story / author, Steven A. Chin; illustrator, David Tamura.
        p.   cm.—(Stories of America)
    Summary: Relates the life and experiences of the Japanese American who defied the order of internment during World War II and took his case as far as the Supreme Court.
        ISBN 0-8114-7236-1 (hardcover) — ISBN 0-8114-8076-3 (softcover)
        1. Japanese Americans—Evacuation and relocation, 1942-1945 —Juvenile literature. 2. Korematsu, Fred, 1919-   —Juvenile literature. 3. Japanese Americans—Biography—Juvenile literature. [1. Japanese Americans—Evacuation and relocation, 1942-1945. 2. Korematsu, Fred, 1919-   . 3. Japanese Americans. 4. World War, 1939-1945—United States. 5. Prejudices.] I. Tamura, David, ill. II. Title. III. Series.
D769.8.A6C4   1993
940.53'1503956073—dc20   92-18086
                                                     CIP
                                                      AC

ISBN 0-8114-7236-1 (Hardcover)
ISBN 0-8114-8076-3 (Softcover)

Introduction
by Alex Haley, General Editor

There once was a comedy skit in which hundreds of people lived in a tall apartment building that a magician had built with his magic. Real people lived in the building, but the building wasn't real. The joke was that whenever anyone stopped believing in the magician's magic, the building would begin to fall. If they believed, the building stood tall and strong.

Democracy is like that. The imaginary building is the American Constitution with its laws, its rights, and its responsibilities. We, the people, are both the magicians and the residents. When we believe in our democracy, it works. When we doubt, it wavers, risking collapse.

The story you are about to read is about one of the times in our history when our faith in our democracy failed us. Our doubts gave way to prejudice, and an entire population of American citizens suffered. It is a story to read with care because its lessons are important.

This book is dedicated to my parents,
Leslie and Ada Chin.

CONTENTS

1

THE REPORT

Karen Korematsu watched her friend Maya Okada nervously approach the front of the class. Their social studies teacher, Mr. Wishnoff, had asked the students to give oral reports about some aspect of World War II. Maya was to present the last report on this spring afternoon in 1967.

Sunlight streamed through the dusty venetian blinds, filling the classroom with a warm, sleepy haze. Students tried to keep their attention focused on Maya, but their eyes and minds wandered. After listening to presentations all period, they were feeling bored and restless. Some gazed idly at the large maps of the United States and

1

the world that hung on one wall of the classroom. In another hour, school would be out, and they could enjoy the rest of this sunny day.

Like most of her classmates, Karen was looking forward to the end of the period. But it wasn't because she was bored. In fact, she was feeling tense as she watched Maya make her way to the front of the class. Karen didn't like talking about World War II. She and Maya were the only Japanese Americans in the class, and their classmates often made fun of them whenever the topic of World War II came up at school.

During the war, Americans had scornfully called their Japanese enemies "Japs" or "Nips" or "Tojo." Such insults were repeated in the many movies and TV shows that were made about the war. Classmates cruelly directed these same offensive words at Karen and Maya, as if *they* were enemies of the United States and not American citizens. It was hard for the girls to understand their classmates' mean behavior. All Karen and Maya knew was that it made them angry, and hurt their feelings—and there was nothing they could do to stop it.

Standing in front of the class in her white blouse and freshly ironed skirt, Maya announced in a clear voice that her report would be about what happened to Japanese Americans living in the United States during World War II.

"Oh, no!" thought Karen worriedly. "Why did she pick that topic? This will only make things worse."

Maya explained that after the Japanese bombed Pearl Harbor, many Americans blamed Japanese Americans for the attack and accused them of acting as spies for the Japanese government. Life became hard for Japanese Americans, especially for those living on the Pacific Coast. People called them ugly names, mistreated them, even attacked them at times. But that was just the beginning.

Three months after the Pearl Harbor bombing, Maya continued, the United States Army ordered all Japanese Americans on the West Coast to be put into internment camps. The Army had been given the power to do this by a special order from President Franklin Roosevelt. The camps were supposed to prevent Japanese Americans from spying or trying to destroy American military property.

As Maya spoke of the internment camps, Karen listened in astonishment. She had never heard of such camps before.

The internment camps were like prisons, her friend explained. There were ten camps in all. Barbed-wire fences ran around the camps, and armed soldiers stood guard to make sure no one escaped. Japanese-American families had to live in cramped barracks as if they were prisoners of war.

Students' eyes focused on Maya as she reported that more than 112,000 Japanese Americans were imprisoned during the war. They were the only group of American citizens singled out in this way, she said. Even though the United States also went to war against Germany and Italy, President Roosevelt did not allow German Americans or Italian Americans to be forced into internment camps.

Several Japanese Americans refused to obey President Roosevelt's order to report to the camps, Maya went on, including a man from California named Korematsu. Korematsu believed the government had no right to force him from his home because of his Japanese heritage. He took his case against Roosevelt's order all the way to the Supreme Court.

Karen gasped when she first heard her family name. "It couldn't be my father," she thought, "not in a million years. Maybe it's one of my uncles."

Then she heard Maya actually say her father's name: "Fred Korematsu." Karen could feel all 34 students in the classroom staring at her, waiting for her to explain the connection between herself and the man. "Is that your father? Is that your father?" everyone, including Mr. Wishnoff, seemed to be asking at once.

Karen didn't know how to respond. She honestly didn't know whether the man was her father or not. What if it *was* her father? Why would he keep this a secret from her? Had he really broken the law?

Karen felt confused, angry, and embarrassed. She didn't know what to think. But she did know that she was mad at Maya for not having told her the topic of her report. How could Maya have presented all that information to the class without warning her beforehand? The remaining minutes it took Maya to finish her report seemed like an eternity to Karen.

When the bell finally rang to end the period, Karen rushed over to Maya.

"Where did you find out about this?" Karen

demanded, clearly upset. "Why didn't you tell me you were going to do this?"

"I thought you already knew," Maya replied, surprised by her friend's harsh tone.

"Well, I didn't," snapped Karen. "I had no idea."

Then Karen headed for the nearest public phone in the school. Inside the phone booth, she grabbed the receiver, jammed a nickel into the coin slot, and quickly dialed her home phone number. How on earth could her parents have kept this from her? she asked herself. *Brring . . . brring . . . brring.* She would get to the bottom of this, and fast. *Brring . . . brring.* Another ten rings and still no answer. No one was home. Karen slammed down the receiver in frustration.

The halls were empty by the time she left the phone booth. All the other students had gone off to their last classes. Still confused and upset, Karen hurried off to hers.

Throughout math class, Karen replayed Maya's report over and over in her mind. She hardly heard a word the teacher was saying. She was hurt that her parents had kept such a big secret from her. She was embarrassed that her father may have been guilty of breaking the law. She was afraid her classmates would now tease her about her father the law-breaker, the Jap spy.

Finally, the bell rang, signaling the end of the day. Karen rushed past her friends mingling in the hallway and raced out the door. She hurried home as fast as she could.

Karen's mother, Kathryn, was in the kitchen preparing dinner when she heard the front door slam.

Karen burst into the kitchen. "Who was this person who challenged the internment?" she shouted. "Was it Dad?"

Kathryn was startled by her daughter's abrupt entrance and rapid-fire questions. Like her father, Karen usually kept her thoughts to herself.

"Is it Dad?" Karen shouted again before her mother could answer.

"Yes, that was your father," said Kathryn.

"Why didn't anyone tell me this?" Karen was more upset than ever.

"Your father didn't want to talk about it," replied Kathryn gently. "It happened a long time ago and it's over."

"Well, are there any papers? Is there anything I can read about it?" Karen asked impatiently.

"Your father doesn't have any documents," answered Kathryn.

Karen was frustrated by the lack of progress she was making. It would be several more hours before her father returned from work. She couldn't wait that long, so she pleaded with her mother to tell all that she knew. They sat down at the kitchen table, and Karen began asking question after question.

At first Kathryn responded haltingly, straining to remember the details of events that had happened years earlier. Kathryn had not even known Fred until the war was over. Slowly, however, she began to remember things that Fred had told her over the years, and she shared those memories with Karen.

Later on, when Fred came home, Karen pressed him to explain why he had resisted internment so many years earlier. But like many Japanese Americans of his generation, Karen's father was reluctant to talk about that part of the past.

Many years before the Pearl Harbor bombing, Japanese immigrants to the United States, including Fred Korematsu's own father, had faced many difficulties. American laws had made it illegal for

9

them to own land or become American citizens. The only jobs they could get were those that most white people didn't want.

Decades later, after the bombing, the situation grew much worse. Fred Korematsu and thousands of other Japanese Americans lost not only their jobs, homes, and belongings, but their ideals of what America was all about as well. It was a time when Japanese Americans were stripped of their honor and betrayed by their own country. To retell the story of that time was to relive it, with all its humiliation, rage, and pain. Yet it was a story that, in the end, had to be told, not only for the sake of personal honor but also for the sake of the country.

2
AMERICA, AMERICA

Fred was born Toyosaburo Korematsu in Oakland, California, in 1919. His parents named him Toyosaburo because it means "richly blessed third son" in Japanese, and "Toy," as his parents nicknamed him, was indeed their third son, for whom they had high hopes. Fred's older brothers were named Hiroshi ("bright scholar") and Takashi ("ambitious one"). The youngest son Jinichi ("perfect virtue") would be born several years later.

Toy and his brothers grew up in a small white house that sat on the grounds of his family's sprawling, 25-acre nursery. Each year his parents raised hundreds of thousands of roses to sell in

11

the busy flower markets of San Francisco, just a few miles away. Raising the beautiful flowers was no easy task, as Toy learned early in his childhood. The Korematsu boys always had plenty of chores to do around the nursery. They had to cut the grass between the ten long, gleaming greenhouses in which the flowers grew. They had to fertilize and water the roses. They had to put away tools and help clean up. Sometimes the work seemed endless.

Having to work at the nursery was especially frustrating when the sun was shining and the air felt cool and inviting. On such days Fred wanted nothing more than to go out and play with his friends. *They* didn't have so many chores to do— why did he? But the answer was clear. The nursery was his parents' life and livelihood, and he was expected to help with the work.

Things became especially hectic with the approach of American holidays such as Valentine's Day and Mother's Day. That's when roses were in huge demand, and sales at the nursery boomed. For months beforehand, the Korematsus groomed and pampered their flowers in preparation for the big selling days. Just before the holidays arrived, Toy's father would hire extra workers to help the family cut and bunch the thousands of flowers that they sold at those times.

Not all holidays meant extra work at the nursery for Toy and his brothers, however. Japanese holidays were different. On those days, the Korematsus took a rare vacation and relaxed with other Japanese in the community.

New Year's Day was Toy's favorite Japanese holiday. For days in advance, his mother would prepare special foods for visitors: crisp batter-fried shrimp (*tempura*), fragrant vegetable stew (*nishime*), flavored rice with vegetables rolled in paper-thin seaweed (*sushi*), and boiled sweet black beans (*kuromame*).

Toy would help his mother pound a special kind of rice into a thick stretchy dough used to make dumplings and soft chewy cakes called *mochi*. The Korematsus always set aside a number of mochi for a special purpose. Toy would stack three of the cakes, place a tangerine on top, and put one of these displays in each of the ten greenhouses for good luck.

Toy also enjoyed going to the yearly picnics that brought together all the local Japanese-American families involved in the nursery business. At the end of each summer, the families

would gather at a park in Oakland for a day of eating and games. As a young boy, Toy loved to compete in the gunny-sack races and egg-carrying contests. He also enjoyed watching the *sumo* wrestling matches.

At the annual summer picnic and on New Year's Day, Toy was very much aware of his Japanese heritage. At home it was the same way. Fred and his brothers were expected to speak Japanese, especially at the dinner table. Fred's father was a strict man and proud of being Japanese. He wanted his sons to take pride in being Japanese, too.

But it was one thing to be Japanese at home and another to be Japanese at school. At school, life was very different for Toy. For starters, no one called him Toyosaburo or even Toy. Everyone called him Fred. One year a teacher had had trouble pronouncing his name, so she called him "Fred." Toy liked his new name and it stuck.

There was only one other Japanese American in the class, which set Fred apart from his classmates. Sometimes they would challenge him to a race or a fight just to see how fast or tough he was. Other times they would look curiously at the delicate rolls of seaweed and rice that his mother occasionally put in his lunch pail.

"What's that you're eating, Fred?" they would ask.

"It's sushi," he would reply patiently. "Want to try some?"

But his classmates just made funny faces. They wouldn't touch it.

Fred soon grew tired of sticking out from the crowd. He often wished that he were like the other students so that he wouldn't be treated differently or teased.

His Japanese-American friends understood these feelings. Fred had many friends at the Japanese Christian church that his family attended. He also played on a Japanese-American football team called the San Leandro Panthers. Fred and his friends were *Nisei*—the first generation of Japanese Americans born in the United States. They all thought of themselves as Americans first, Japanese second.

Their parents, on the other hand, were *Issei*—immigrants. Like most immigrants, their first tie was to their homeland, Japan. Fred's parents accepted the fact that their sons had adopted many American ways and had even taken American names—Hiroshi was known as "Hi," Takashi as "Harry," Toy as "Fred," and Jinichi as "Joe." Sometimes, though, the boys' American ways caused problems.

When Fred and his brothers did not want their parents to understand what they were saying, for example, they would speak English instead of Japanese. In English, the boys could complain as much as they wanted about the chores they had to do around the nursery. This infuriated Fred's father.

"Speak Japanese so I can understand you!" he would yell in Japanese.

As much work as their father gave the boys to do around the nursery, however, he never lost sight of the importance of school. School would be his sons' pathway to success in America. Besides getting good grades, he encouraged the boys to participate in school activities.

One of Fred's favorite school activities was sports. In high school Fred made the school's tennis team. Through tennis and other sports, Fred developed friendships with his classmates.

When Fred and his friends graduated from high school in 1938, they looked forward to heading out into the world on their own. After all, they were adults now, with high hopes for the future. Fred planned to leave the nursery behind and attend college in Los Angeles to study business.

But his plans were soon dashed. Fred's father could not afford to help a third son pay tuition; he was already putting Hi and Harry through college.

Fred looked for a job so that he could pay for school himself. The only jobs he could find were working as a house servant or selling fruit at a fruit stand, neither of which paid very well. Still, for three months he struggled to work and attend school at the same time. Doing both, however, proved to be too much. Bitterly disappointed, Fred returned to Oakland. For the next two years, he worked at the nursery that he had hoped to leave behind forever.

3
PEARL HARBOR

When the new year dawned on January 1, 1941, the Korematsus, like other Americans, found little to celebrate. Instead, they were worried. Much of the world was at war, and the United States was finding it increasingly difficult to remain neutral in the widening conflict.

In 1940, President Franklin Roosevelt had agreed to provide war supplies to Great Britain. Britain was fighting against a powerful Nazi Germany that had already conquered virtually all of Europe. At the same time, Japan was rolling up conquests of its own in Asia and across the Pacific.

The world seemed to be growing more dangerous by the day. War now seemed imminent to Americans.

In September, Congress had passed a law stating that men would be drafted into the armed forces. Fred and five of his high school friends didn't wait to be drafted. Out of a sense of patriotism, they went down to the local post office one day in June 1941 to volunteer for service. There they joined a line of eager young men standing before a desk cluttered with forms. As they waited for the slow-moving line to advance, Fred and his friends joked and teased one another. It helped take their minds off the big step they were about to take.

At last their turn came. One by one, the recruiting officer gave out applications to each of Fred's friends. Fred held out his hand expectantly, but the officer looked past him as if he wasn't there. Fred glanced at his friends and shrugged. Once more he held out his hand, but again the officer ignored him.

"We have orders not to accept you," the officer finally told Fred.

It was humiliating to be rejected outright, especially in front of his friends and all these gaping strangers. Flustered, Fred asked why he could not be accepted. The officer just told him to step aside. Others were waiting to enlist.

Why was he being rejected? Fred asked himself. But in his heart, he knew the reason. His rejection had nothing to do with his abilities. It had to do with his race. All Fred's friends were white. Fred, the one Japanese American in the recruiting office, was the only person not given an application.

Fred tried not to let the rejection discourage him. He knew that tensions between Japan and the United States were high. Ugly newspaper headlines about "Jap" victories and about the "Yellow Peril" in Asia fueled local prejudice against Japanese Americans. Things would settle down before long, he told himself, and then he'd get his chance to serve his country.

In the meantime, Fred took a job as a welder at an Oakland shipyard, helping to build huge merchant ships. He worked hard, and his boss steadily gave him more and more responsibilities. Fred viewed his welding job as a way to help his country prepare for war.

One morning when he arrived at work, however, Fred went to punch in at the time clock, only to discover that his time card was missing.

Without it, he could not begin work. Why would anyone take my time card? he wondered.

Fred walked over to his union office to report that his time card was missing. Like all welders at the shipyard, he belonged to the Boilermakers' Union. The union pledged to protect the rights of its members.

Fred bounded up a flight of stairs to the office and knocked on the door. A union official opened the door and stared at him coolly.

"I can't find my time card," said Fred. "Do you know what might have happened to it?"

The official glared at him for a moment, then slammed the door in his face without saying a word. It took a moment for Fred to realize the harsh truth. He'd been fired, and the union wasn't going to do a thing about it.

Fred stood outside the office, stunned and speechless. He could think of only one reason for losing his job this way: he was an American of Japanese descent.

He shook his head grimly at the cold injustice of being fired. But there was no one to turn to for help. Even his own union would not stand up for him.

As he walked back down the stairs, Fred felt

anger simmering inside him. This was unfair. Why blame *him* for Japan's aggression in the Pacific? He'd had nothing to do with it.

He headed over to his locker and packed up his smudged overalls, heavy metal helmet, and welding equipment. Waving goodbye to some friends, Fred trudged out of the shipyard. No one tried to console him. Neither his boss nor his union wanted people of Japanese descent working at the shipyard, even if they were Americans. That was the part that truly troubled Fred. Why didn't it seem to matter that he was an American citizen, with American rights?

Fred was not out of work for long. Welders were in great demand because American industries were in high gear, producing goods for the war effort. He found a new job quickly.

But he had been working at his new job for just one week when a boss who had been out of town when Fred was hired saw him.

"Hey, you!" he yelled. "You're Japanese! I don't want you working here!" He fired Fred on the spot.

Fred had now lost two jobs because he was of Japanese descent. What would happen if Japan and the United States actually went to war? He didn't like to think about that possibility. There was no telling how bad things might get for Japanese Americans, especially for Issei like his parents who still dearly loved the homeland they had left so long ago.

Then came a day that Fred would never forget—Sunday, December 7, 1941.

It was a beautiful, crisp winter morning. After a quick breakfast, Fred jumped into his old gray Pontiac and drove over to pick up his girlfriend Ida Boitano. The two had been dating for nearly three years, much to the displeasure of Ida's parents.

It wasn't that they disliked Fred's personality or what he did for a living. It was his race. Like many white Americans, the Boitanos believed that people of Japanese descent were inferior and unfit to mix with white people. Mrs. Boitano made her views clear to Ida, but her daughter paid her no mind.

Fred and Ida headed up into the hills above Oakland. They often drove around the Oakland hills on Sundays. It was one of Fred's favorite places because of the breathtaking view of San Francisco Bay and the San Francisco skyline.

Fred parked the car in a spot with a lovely

view. A Tommy Dorsey song played softly on the car radio. In the seclusion of the shady green woods, Fred and Ida talked about someday getting married and having children. Everything seemed so quiet and peaceful.

Suddenly, the music was cut short and a breathless radio announcer shouted, "Pearl Harbor has been attacked by the Japanese!"

Jolted, Fred and Ida looked at each other in shock.

Fred was stunned by the news. How could they bomb Pearl Harbor? he thought in anger and disbelief. Then he began to think about how the Boitanos and other white people might react. Would he and his family somehow be blamed for this?

For a long time Fred and Ida sat numbly in the car, not knowing what to say.

"Maybe we'd better go home," Fred suggested at last.

They drove in silence. Although both had known for some time that war was likely to break out, they rarely brought up the subject. It was easier to pretend that everything was going to be all right. Now, however, they could pretend no longer.

Fred took Ida to her house, then rushed home to see if his family had heard the terrible news. He burst in the door and found everyone crowded around the kitchen table, listening to the radio. Fred saw the fear on their faces. He had never seen his mother look so scared before.

For the rest of that afternoon, the Korematsus stayed close to the radio, listening for more news about the bombing. Their minds were filled with questions. What would it mean for the United States to go to war against Japan and its allies? How would the war affect their relatives living in Japan? How would the war affect *them*?

All across the country that fateful afternoon, Japanese-American families braced themselves for the worst. Issei like Fred's parents knew that the American government had always looked upon Japanese people in America with suspicion and contempt, even in times of peace. Nisei like Fred had faced mockery for being Japanese, even though they were American citizens. What would happen to them now that Japan and America were at war?

4
"A JAP'S A JAP"

Before the smoke had cleared over Pearl Harbor, Federal Bureau of Investigation agents began sweeping through Japanese-American communities along the West Coast. Stories quickly circulated among Japanese Americans of nighttime visits from grim-faced federal agents.

The FBI agents were gruff and officious as they examined each family's belongings. They asked question after question. Who sent you this letter postmarked from Hiroshima? When? Why? The agents' stern questions flustered Issei. "It's just a letter from a cousin," they would try to explain.

The agents asked everyone what organizations

they belonged to and what newspapers they read. They asked, "Do you feel loyalty towards the Japanese emperor?" They seized flashlights and radio equipment, thinking that perhaps such items might be used to signal Japanese ships or fighter planes. They seized "suspect" pieces of evidence, such as documents written in Japanese or Japanese-language family Bibles. Often they seized the men of the house, escorting them off into the night for further questioning.

Although the FBI agents never came to Fred's house, his parents were frightened. They saw agents take some of their friends to jail. They wondered if they would be next. Dinnertime at the Korematsus' was now hushed and somber. Fred's father, who usually loved talking at the dinner table about the good old days in Japan, suddenly had little to say.

Fred wondered what private thoughts were going through his father's mind. The man had spent almost forty years of his life—more than half a lifetime—on American soil. During that time he had been denied citizenship, denied the right to own property like any American because of his Japanese heritage. And now, on top of everything, he faced being treated like a criminal.

Fred wondered if his father ever thought about uprooting the family and going "home" to Japan. But where *was* home these days, anyway? For Fred, it certainly wasn't Japan. He had never even been there.

FBI agents were only one of the problems that Fred's family faced after the bombing of Pearl Harbor. Neighbors who once were friendly with the Korematsus stopped talking with them after the Japanese attack.

One neighbor did more than that. Next door to the Korematsu nursery was a foundry that produced machinery. For more than thirty years the Korematsus had gotten along well with the foundry's owner. They would chat together pleasantly and do small favors for one another. After Pearl Harbor, though, the owner set up a huge spotlight that lit up the Korematsus' house at night. A guard stood on top of the foundry's tower to watch the Korematsus' every move. He noted who came and went, what cars drove into the driveway, and how long visitors stayed. The foundry owner was taking no chances. The Korematsus might be spies.

One night Fred stepped onto his porch to smoke a cigarette. As he lit a match, a voice boomed out of the still darkness.

"Are you signaling someone? Who are you signaling?"

Fred was startled at first. Then he realized it was the voice of the foundry guard. The man thought Fred might be trying to contact the Japanese navy using matches! Fred would have laughed at the ridiculous idea if he hadn't been so annoyed.

Anti-Japanese sentiment, which had been a part of life for as long as Fred and his family could remember, seemed to grow stronger day by day. White businessmen and farmers began calling for the removal of every Japanese man, woman, and child from the West Coast. Newspapers took up the call for removal. One declared: "A viper is nonetheless a viper wherever the egg is hatched, so a Japanese American—born of Japanese parents—grows up to be a Japanese, not an American."

On February 20, 1942, newspapers reported that President Roosevelt had signed a document called Executive Order 9066. The order gave the United States military the right to expel "any or all persons" it wished from areas deemed off-limits for reasons of military security. Nowhere in the document were Japanese or Japanese

Americans mentioned, but everyone seemed to know that they were the targets of the order.

Rumors of mass arrests, removal, and imprisonment spread rapidly throughout the Japanese-American community. No one could say for sure what was going to happen as a result of Executive Order 9066, or who would be affected. One thing seemed clear, however: the man responsible for carrying out the order was no friend of Japanese Americans. Lieutenant General John L. De Witt had identified all Japanese and Japanese Americans as "a dangerous element." If people tried to make a point about Japanese Americans being United States citizens, he would have none of it. "A Jap's a Jap," he would declare. "It makes no difference whether he is an American; theoretically he is still a Japanese."

No one knew how far De Witt's plans would go. Japanese-American families wondered whether they should pack up and leave their communities or stay behind to protect the businesses and homes they had worked a lifetime to build. People felt helpless and frustrated. Their entire lives were at the mercy of a handful of government officials.

One day in late March, Fred spotted some soldiers driving toward his house. He froze, his mind racing. Would the soldiers stop here? What would they do? What would happen to his family? When the jeep pulled up in front of the nursery and a soldier stepped out, Fred's heart began to pound. But instead of coming toward the house, the soldier walked over to a nearby telephone pole and posted a long white notice on it.

As soon as the soldiers drove away, Fred ran out of the house to read the notice. It was a curfew notice. "All alien Japanese, all alien Germans, all alien Italians, and *all persons of Japanese ancestry*" had to remain in their homes between eight o'clock at night and six o'clock in the morning or face arrest, it warned. Now it was clear that the government looked upon *all* those of Japanese heritage, United States citizens or not, as The Enemy.

In practical terms, Fred realized the curfew meant he could no longer see his girlfriend in the evenings. Even though Ida was of Italian descent, she was not The Enemy. Fred was. Being Japanese American made him so.

The curfew made Fred and his family even more worried—and they were not alone. No one in the Japanese-American community knew what to expect next. If they kept the curfew, would they and their families finally be left in peace? Was the curfew the worst of it all? Or was this only the beginning?

5
THE ROUNDUP

Early on the morning of May 2, 1942, many people were still in bed, enjoying the luxury of a Saturday off from work. Fred's parents, though, were already hard at work in their greenhouses. They were preparing their roses for the Mother's Day holiday just two weeks away.

As they worked, Army jeeps once again came rumbling through the community. Soldiers began posting official notices on telephone poles around the Oakland area. This time, though, the worst had come. This time, the innocent-looking sheets of white paper announced that "All persons of Japanese ancestry" were to evacuate their homes immediately. "Dispose of your homes and property.

Wind up your business," the posters instructed. "One sea bag of bedding, two suitcases of clothing allowed per person." On the following Saturday, May 9, they were to report to authorities with their belongings, prepared to move into "assembly centers."

Many Japanese Americans were numb with shock as they read the notice. Some spoke angrily of the injustice that they were powerless to stop. Others cried in distress.

One week to wrap up a lifetime! Where should they begin? Fred's parents argued over what to do with their house and the nursery. What would happen to the nursery and all the beautiful flowers ready for Mother's Day? Where would they store all their belongings? The precious family photographs . . . the family heirlooms . . . the fragile china . . . .

And what should they pack to bring with them? Should they take heavy wool sweaters or light cotton clothing? The answer depended on where they were going—but that was something no one knew. Should they pack food supplies in case there wasn't enough food where they were going? No one could answer that question either. It was a maddening dilemma. Their future lives

might well depend on what they put inside their two suitcases and one sea bag, but there was no way to know what things they might need.

Tempers flared. Tears flowed. There was too much to do and too little time. No one could say how long they would be gone—or if they would ever be allowed to return home again.

Fortunately, Fred's father found a warehouse where the family could store its belongings. He arranged to have a German-American family take care of the nursery after he and his family were taken away. In exchange for watching over the house and the nursery, the family was to keep any money it made from selling the Korematsus' roses.

White neighbors came by the Korematsu nursery looking for evacuation bargains. They had read newspaper articles about the fabulous sales Japanese Americans were having. "JAP TOWN SELLS OUT," announced the *San Francisco Chronicle*. "Along Post Street between Octavia and Webster, you can buy anything from a pool table to a begonia plant cheap," the newspaper declared.

"Can I have this wheelbarrow?" asked one man who came snooping into the Korematsus' yard. "How about these tires?"

"No, they're not for sale," said Fred angrily. He was tired of people taking advantage of his family's misfortune. They reminded him of vultures swooping down on helpless victims.

Fred was forced to sell his car because he had no place to store it. Giving up the old gray Pontiac would hurt. The car meant so much to him. Like most young Americans, Fred had dreamed of owning his own car since he was a child. When he had bought the Pontiac, it became a symbol of his independence. Now that symbol was about to be taken away.

When a man came by the house and offered to buy the car for a mere two hundred dollars, Fred couldn't believe his ears.

"But I bought this car a year and a half ago for eight hundred dollars," he protested.

"You're lucky to get this much," the man replied with a smirk. "This is war, you know."

Fred controlled his anger. He had no choice but to take the man's offer. It was one of the hardest things he ever had to do.

While his family busily packed up belongings and prepared to leave the nursery, Fred thought about what he should do. If he evacuated and went to the assembly center with his family, he would have to leave Ida behind—and they did not want to separate. On the other hand, if he didn't follow the evacuation orders, he could be arrested as a criminal.

Fred and Ida discussed their options at length and finally agreed upon a plan. Fred would not go with his parents. Instead, he and Ida would leave California as soon as possible and head east, maybe to Nevada. Once they got out of California, Fred thought they would be safe, because the removal order under Executive Order 9066 affected only the states on the Pacific Coast. He and Ida would get married and move to the Midwest, where Japanese Americans were still able, they hoped, to live relatively peaceful lives.

Fred waited for the right moment to discuss his plans with his parents. Then he told them of his intentions.

"I'll leave for Nevada before the deadline to evacuate," Fred promised. He also reminded them of friends they knew who were heading inland to avoid the assembly centers, just as he was planning to do.

But the elderly Korematsus were dismayed. In this time of persecution, the last thing they wanted to see happen was the breakup of their precious family. It was all they had left in the world.

They were also concerned about Fred's safety. Like most Japanese Americans, they had heard reports of Japanese Americans facing terrible hostility as they tried to move inland. Gas stations, motels, and restaurants were refusing to serve them. One diner had even posted a sign reading: "This restaurant poisons both rats and Japs." Armed patrolmen were turning back families at the Nevada, Arizona, and Kansas state lines. "The Japs live like rats, breed like rats and act like rats," declared the governor of Idaho. "I don't want them coming into Idaho."

But much as the Korematsus hated to lose their son and worried for his safety, they knew that he cared deeply for Ida Boitano and had a chance to live a better life with her far away from California. After what seemed like hours of discussion, the Korematsus reluctantly gave Fred their blessing.

"Go ahead," said his mother. "But be careful!"

There was no time to lose. After saying good-bye to his parents and brothers, Fred quietly moved into a cheap boarding house nearby. He was on his own.

6
A DOUBLE LIFE

On the morning of May 9, 1942, the deadline to evacuate, the Korematsus prepared to report to the nearby Civil Control Station without Fred. They squeezed a few last belongings into their sea bags and suitcases. Then they attached numbered tags to their bags and coats. From now on they would be known by the family number assigned to them, rather than by their name. Fred's father took a last look at the nursery that had been his life for much of his 64 years. Fred's mother wept as she locked up the house, knowing that she might never see it again.

All around the Oakland community, the same scene was repeated over and over again as people tearfully said goodbye to friends, homes, and businesses. At the Civil Control Station the families were met by soldiers standing guard with rifles. Buses idled at the curb, waiting to take the families away.

One by one, family numbers were called out, and families and their belongings were put aboard the buses. The doors closed with a hiss, gears ground noisily, and the buses pulled away.

White Americans who had pushed for the removal of Japanese Americans had gotten what they wanted. A community that had made its presence felt in the Oakland area for over forty years vanished in a single day, forcibly uprooted by the government. All across town, shops owned by Japanese Americans were deserted, their hastily scrawled "Evacuation Sale!" signs still taped to the windows. Homes had new white tenants in them or were padlocked and still. As of May 10, 1942, it was against the law for Japanese Americans to be living in Oakland or any other city on the West Coast.

Fred, however, was still living at the boarding house near his parents' home. He had not left for Nevada as planned, because Ida had begun having second thoughts about leaving her family.

By remaining in the area, Fred was challenging the evacuation law. To avoid being recognized as a Japanese person, he told people he was of Spanish-Hawaiian descent. He carefully changed the name on his draft card to read "Clyde Sarah," and erased from the card the words "enemy alien."

While he waited for Ida to make up her mind about leaving, Fred used his false name to get a welding job at a trailer company in Berkeley. Every other day he met Ida after work. She was working at a biscuit factory and as a piano teacher at home.

For several weeks, Fred felt as if life had almost returned to normal—except when he read the newspaper. Every day the newspaper seemed to carry stories about the "Yellow Peril" and new "Jap" victories in Southeast Asia. One day he read an article about a young Japanese-American man who had been arrested for not evacuating. The story scared Fred. He realized that he, too, could be turned in at any moment by some "patriot." But Fred pushed such doubts and fears to the back of his mind. He refused to let such worries keep him from living a normal, free life.

On May 30, three weeks after his parents had

been evacuated, Fred made plans with Ida to go shopping. They arranged to meet in the afternoon on a corner in San Leandro. Fred arrived before Ida and decided to buy some cigarettes at the drugstore across the street. It was a store Fred must have shopped in before because an alert clerk recognized him.

"Hey, you're Japanese!" the clerk exclaimed.

Alarmed, Fred hurriedly paid for his cigarettes and rushed out of the drugstore. He was relieved to find Ida waiting for him across the street. After a quick greeting, he grabbed her hand, and they started walking briskly down the street.

When they reached the corner of Estudillo Street and MacArthur Boulevard, Fred spotted a police patrol car heading their way. Fred's stride quickened. His grip tightened around Ida's hand. He prayed that the officers in the patrol car would not see him.

Maybe they're not even looking for me, he tried to convince himself, as his heart pounded wildly.

But the patrol car pulled up to Fred and Ida and stopped. As an officer slowly climbed from the car, Fred considered running away, then decided it was best to stay put.

The officer, A.B. Poulsen, asked Fred for some identification.

"What are you doing here?" Officer Poulsen asked as he examined the draft card that Fred had altered.

Fred explained that he and his girlfriend were going shopping.

"Are you Japanese?" the officer asked.

"I'm American," Fred answered.

Suspecting that Fred was of Japanese descent, Officer Poulsen put Fred and Ida in the back of his car and took them to the Alameda County Jail for further questioning. At the jail Ida and Fred were put in separate rooms and questioned. The police were not concerned that Ida was of Italian descent or that her parents had come from Italy. They were interested only in her relationship with their suspect, "Clyde Sarah."

After several hours, an exhausted Ida left the jail. Fred, however, was still being questioned. The questioning made him nervous and angry at the same time. Why was he being interrogated as if he were some kind of enemy?

Hoping to avoid arrest, Fred steadfastly refused to reveal his true identity. Then an FBI

agent, Oliver Mansfield, was brought in to question him. More nervous than ever now, Fred kept insisting that he was not Japanese.

Agent Mansfield's relentless questioning only made Fred more afraid of what would happen if the agent discovered that he was of Japanese descent. Fred felt that he had no choice but to lie. He told the FBI agent that he was Spanish Hawaiian and that he had been born in Las Vegas, Nevada. He also said that his parents were dead—they had been killed in a fire when their house burned to the ground.

During a break in questioning, Fred noticed a woman talking to Officer Poulsen and pointing at Fred. Nervously, he wondered what she was saying about him. His hands began to sweat.

When Agent Mansfield returned to resume questioning, it immediately became clear that the woman had recognized Fred. It was no use, Fred realized. He could no longer avoid arrest.

Wearily, Fred admitted to Agent Mansfield that his real name was Fred Korematsu. His parents had gone to an assembly center three weeks earlier, but he had remained behind with the intention of going to Nevada with his fiancée.

After his confession, the police arrested Fred for violating the evacuation order. He was finger-printed, photographed, and given a criminal record. Then he was put in jail.

7
A TEST CASE

Fred barely slept at all during his first night in jail. His mind was jumbled with all sorts of thoughts and emotions. He felt scared and lonely and humiliated. What would his parents think when they found out he had been arrested? He hated to think about what his father would say when he heard the news.

Mostly, Fred felt angry about being treated like a criminal. Was he or wasn't he an American citizen? Was he or wasn't he guaranteed certain rights under the Constitution of the United States of America? Fred vowed to fight his arrest, although he didn't know exactly how yet.

Fred's arrest made newspaper headlines. "Jap

Spy Arrested," screamed one headline. Fred instantly became famous, for reasons that dismayed and angered him. Never again would he be just an ordinary citizen. Now he would always be Fred Korematsu, the criminal.

One lawyer took great interest in the newspaper stories about Fred and his arrest. His name was Ernest Besig. Besig worked with a group of lawyers who made it their business to defend the civil rights of Americans. The group was called the American Civil Liberties Union (ACLU). The ACLU had chapters across the country, with a main office in New York City. Ernest Besig was in charge of the group's office in northern California.

Besig believed that the government's decision to treat Japanese Americans as criminals was gravely wrong. It violated basic principles of the Constitution. Yet, in order to challenge the government's actions as being unconstitutional, he needed to find a Japanese American who was willing to take the government to court over the issue. When he read about Fred in the newspaper, Besig thought that Fred might be just the person he was looking for.

Besig came to visit Fred in jail. Fred did not

know who this stranger was or what he wanted, but he listened quietly.

"This is a very important case," Besig explained to Fred. "The government is discriminating against you and other Japanese Americans."

Fred was heartened by Besig's words. At last, here was someone who saw things as he did. But what could Besig and his organization do about the situation?

Besig said the ACLU would provide Fred with a lawyer to help him fight his case. By taking his case to court, Fred would create a "test case" that would force courts to rule on the legality of the discrimination against Japanese Americans.

"Will you be the test case?" Besig asked Fred.

Fred was thrilled. He had wanted to take his case to court, but had given up hope that anyone else would help him fight his battle. Eagerly he accepted Besig's offer.

Besig warned Fred that it would be a very long and tough fight. The American public and many politicians, including the President of the United States, believed that the Japanese-American community was dangerous and had to be imprisoned. Fred assured him that he was ready for the fight. Then Fred's new ally left to begin preparing their case.

Besig had not expected that their first battle would be with the heads of his own organization. When board members of the ACLU heard that Besig had taken Fred's case, they ordered him to drop the case immediately. Some board members were friendly with people in government who wanted to imprison Japanese Americans. They did not want to embarrass their government friends by challenging Executive Order 9066.

But Ernest Besig refused to give in to the ACLU board's demands. "We don't intend to trim our sails," he wrote back to the board. Then he hired a fiery young lawyer named Wayne Collins to represent Fred in court. A week later at Fred's bail hearing, Besig paid five thousand dollars to the court so that Fred would not have to wait in jail for his trial.

At last Fred was free again. As he and Besig walked out of the courthouse, Fred looked around, squinting against the bright sunlight. A blue sky yawned overhead. Pigeons soared over the nearby rooftops. Buses and cars crawled along Market Street. People bustled along the sidewalks. Fred took a deep breath, thinking how wonderful it felt to be free. Even if a judge later decided that the government was "right" after all, at least he was free for now.

Fred took a few more steps, then suddenly felt the looming presence of four men. Military police. His breath caught in his throat.

With weapons drawn, the police grabbed him as he stood there. As Fred protested that his lawyer had paid the five thousand dollars bail, Besig demanded they let Fred go. But the military police said that they had orders to take Fred away.

Shoving Fred into their jeep, they told him that he was headed for the Tanforan Assembly Center, the center where other members of his family were being held as prisoners.

8
LONELY DAYS

Sitting in the jeep, flanked by military police, Fred made the journey that the rest of his family and other members of Oakland's Japanese-American community had made more than a month ago. As the jeep crossed the San Francisco Bay Bridge and wound its way through the busy streets of San Francisco, Fred watched the passing scene. He saw workers going to their offices, shoppers entering stores, children playing games and riding bikes. Being able to move about freely was something everyone took for granted. For Fred, though, such freedom was beginning to seem like an impossible dream.

After an hour's drive, the jeep pulled into the

Tanforan Assembly Center. Before Tanforan had become a temporary holding ground for thousands of Japanese-American families, it had been a busy race track. It still resembled the race track it had been—but it also looked like the prison it now was.

A barbed-wire fence surrounded the complex, and armed guards manned watchtowers around the track. Soldiers with rifles and fixed bayonets opened the gates to let the jeep into the parking lot. The jeep stopped in front of the old grandstand building, and Fred was taken inside to the "processing" area. There, prison officials frisked him from head to toe for weapons and then completed the necessary paperwork.

As they filled out the required forms, prison officials offered to place Fred with his family in the barrack they had been assigned. But Fred asked instead to be given his own room far away from everyone else. He was afraid to face his family. Surely they had heard of his arrest by now. Surely his father would be very angry at him for breaking his word and getting in trouble with the law.

With a final stamp, Fred's paperwork was complete. A guide appeared to take Fred to his new quarters. As they walked, Fred looked in horrified amazement at the conditions in which people were living. Passing through the grandstand building, he caught sight of the immense dormitory that had been created in the windowless gloom. Hundreds of beds lined the floor, providing no privacy whatsoever. More than three hundred single men now lived there.

Fred and his guide made their way out into the piercing sunlight and headed toward the track. As far as his eyes could see, Fred looked out upon row after row of flimsy-looking barracks covered with tar paper. People were everywhere—children playing in the dusty rows between barracks, women hanging up laundry to dry, men making tables and chairs out of scrap lumber.

Then his guide turned and headed toward what clearly had been horse stalls. Fred couldn't believe it. Surely the government wouldn't be using horse stalls to house people! But it was true. Fred's guide led him to his "apartment"—a horse stall far from where other people were living.

As they walked in through the splintered half-door, Fred smelled the unmistakable odor of horse manure. Frowning at the overpowering smell, he looked around. Sunlight barely penetrated a filthy window. A single light bulb hung from the ceiling, casting a weak pall of light through the dusty stall.

He shook his head. His prison cell had been much cleaner and more comfortable than this. But now, supposedly free on bail, he was being forced to live here in a *horse stall*. Disgusted, Fred sat down on a sagging cot that was pushed up against a wall. The "mattress" beneath him was made of straw and crackled with his every move.

Breathing through his mouth to keep from smelling the odor of the horse manure, Fred took a closer look at his new prison cell. The rough wooden walls had been hastily whitewashed, but they could not hide the filth. Here and there cobwebs and horse hairs were perfectly preserved under the coating of whitewash. Against the wall, he could make out horseshoe marks where the stall's previous inmates had kicked to protest their imprisonment.

How could the government do this to us? Fred kept asking himself over and over. Getting arrested and going to prison had been a nightmare in itself. But this! He hadn't even broken the law to earn such treatment! Had the country gone mad?

A knock at the door interrupted Fred's angry thoughts. It was Hi, his eldest brother. Fred was happy to see him, despite his fears of having to face the family. He wondered how his brother had found out that he was here. How much did his family know of the circumstances that had brought him to Tanforan? Cautiously, he asked Hi if they had heard about his arrest.

"Of course," Hi replied. "It's in all the newspapers. Now come see the rest of the family," he said briskly. "You can stay with us."

Fred nodded with relief. Together they started on the long walk to the barrack where the Korematsus lived. As they walked along the dusty paths, Hi asked question after question. Why hadn't Fred left town when he was supposed to? What was it like in jail? How was he treated?

Fred told Hi about getting arrested and his lonely nights in jail and about Ernest Besig. He told Hi that with Besig's help, he planned to fight his arrest.

Outside the family's doorway, Fred paused to take a deep breath. Then he opened the flimsy wooden door and went inside. Across the small darkened room, Fred saw his mother. She immediately burst into tears. She had been so worried about him.

At first, Fred's father stared at him sternly. Then he exploded, making clear just how upset he was with Fred for having broken both the law and his promise to leave California immediately. The entire family had been shamed by Fred's arrest, he shouted.

Fred sat in silence, eyes fixed on the floor, as his father continued to yell at him. He did not dare say that he planned to fight his arrest. His father would call him a troublemaker and get even angrier, Fred thought, if that was possible. Better to remain silent.

Later, after his father had calmed down, Fred took a look around his family's new "apartment." There wasn't much to see. The room where Fred's family lived was bigger than his horse stall, but not by much. At least it didn't smell. And his brothers had done a good job papering over the cracks between the boards in the walls so that less wind blew through. For partitions, they had hung Army blankets from the ceiling with rope. Fred's mother had made a blanketed-off "room" just for him.

Fred's brothers took him around the camp to show him where the mess hall, bathroom facilities, and camp store were. He quickly learned that long lines were an aggravating part of daily life in Tanforan. Before each meal, thousands of people waited in lines that snaked around the block. Afterwards, they waited in still more lines to wash their dishes. They waited in line to use the communal showers. They waited in line to buy goods at the camp store—and often found the store shelves empty when they finally reached the front of the line.

Tanforan was no better than jail. There were nightly curfews. Roll calls were held twice a day. Camp police roamed the grounds, watching for suspicious activity. At night, searchlights swept the camp, looking for people trying to escape. Unlike prison inmates, however, the prisoners of this camp had done nothing to warrant their imprisonment.

A few days after Fred arrived at Tanforan, Hi arranged a meeting with some of the younger men in camp to talk about whether Fred should take his case to court. It was a lively debate. Some men said that challenging the evacuation order would be viewed as unpatriotic. Above all,

they wanted to prove to other Americans that Japanese Americans were loyal citizens. Fred's case, they argued, would only make Japanese Americans look disloyal.

Others disagreed. They felt that, as citizens, they shouldn't have to prove their loyalty. No other group had to do so.

But most of the men in the room agreed that challenging the government would make life more difficult for everyone in the camps. By continuing to fight, Fred would be making trouble for all Japanese Americans.

Fred listened in silence to the debate. In the end, the men said it was up to Fred to decide what he would do, although they made it clear that they disapproved of the idea of going to court. But Fred had already made up his mind. He was going to take his case to court.

Fred's decision isolated him even further in Tanforan. His relationship with his parents was already strained because of his arrest. People viewed him as a troublemaker and avoided talking to him. They were scared that they, too, might be seen as troublemakers, just for associating with him.

Fred had never felt so lonely in his life. Even

Ida had given up on him. Shortly after arriving in Tanforan, Fred had received a letter from her. Ida wrote that she thought it best to end their relationship. Fred was heartbroken. He found himself at the lowest point of his life—imprisoned, without a job, without friends, and now, without his fiancée.

With little else to occupy his thoughts now, Fred spent most of the long, hot summer thinking about his case. As the date of Fred's trial drew near, Ernest Besig came to visit him at Tanforan. The Tanforan visiting room was just like the ones in jail—prisoners sat on one side of a table, visitors on the other. All packages were searched by guards before being handed over to prisoners.

Sitting at the visitors' table, Fred handed Besig a statement that he had taken great care to write. The statement expressed all the rage that had been building up inside him over the past year.

"Assembly Camps were for Dangerous Enemy Aliens and Citizens," Fred noted. This description didn't apply to anyone he knew, not to his family, friends, or neighbors—and not to himself.

Fred's statement went on. "People should have a fair trial" and a chance to "defend their loyalty at court in a democratic way." In this situation, people "were placed in imprisonment without any fair trial!"

Civics classes had hammered into Fred's mind that all Americans were entitled to a speedy and fair trial. He also had been told that Americans could not have their freedom or property taken from them without a trial. What, then, had happened to the rights of Japanese Americans?

Fred pointed out that German and Italian agents had been arrested on the East Coast. But no one had argued that all German or Italian Americans should be "corralled under armed guard like the Japanese." Fred then posed a key question, knowing full well its answer: "Is this a racial issue?"

If evacuation was not a racial issue, Fred concluded, then Japanese Americans should be granted a "fair trial to prove their loyalty! Also," he added, thinking of his parents, "there are many loyal aliens who can prove their loyalty to America, and they must be given fair trial and treatment!"

Fred hoped that his test case would help give all Japanese Americans the "fair trial" they deserved. But only time would tell.

Ernest Besig smiled as he read Fred's document. Fred was clearly ready to fight his battle in court.

On September 8, 1942, Fred and his lawyer, Wayne Collins, finally appeared in court. At the trial, Fred told Judge Adolphus St. Sure that he was a loyal American, not a spy for Japan. "As a citizen of the United States," he said, "I am ready, willing and able to bear arms for this country."

Although Judge St. Sure was impressed with Fred's testimony, he found Fred guilty of not obeying the military order to evacuate. But he did not sentence Fred to prison. Instead, he gave Fred five years' probation. For any citizen of non-Japanese descent, this sentence would have meant virtual freedom. For Fred, however, it meant returning to the prison of Tanforan.

Wayne Collins immediately filed for another trial. He believed that Fred had a chance to overturn Judge St. Sure's ruling in a higher court, the Court of Appeals.

9

"THE JEWEL OF THE DESERT"

One week after Fred appeared in court, the government began a massive drive to evacuate families from Tanforan. Once more, people were ordered to pack up their belongings. The camp buzzed with unanswered questions about where the inmates at Tanforan were going and what would happen to them.

Soon the Korematsus and other prisoners were crammed aboard a creaky old train. For the next two and a half days they lurched and chugged eastward—through the familiar, lush farming region beyond San Francisco, up the towering Sierra Nevada Mountains, and into the unfamiliar, barren deserts of Nevada. Fred had finally made it to Nevada—but not in the way he had hoped or planned. It was the farthest he had ever traveled from home.

The train cabin was hot and stuffy. The lurching motion of the train and the lack of air made many people sick to their stomachs. Yet there was no escape. Although the train made frequent stops along the way, passengers were not allowed to get off. The train was a moving prison.

At last the train pulled up at a small town in the middle of the desert. "Delta, Utah," the signs announced. Everyone was told to get off the train. The rumpled, travel-weary prisoners stumbled out, glad to be breathing fresh air for the first time in three days.

All too soon, however, they were ordered into waiting buses, escorted by armed guards. After a long ride along deeply rutted dirt roads, rows of long black barracks suddenly appeared on the bare horizon ahead. This was Topaz, the internment camp officials had nicknamed "the Jewel of the Desert."

Topaz was one of ten internment camps that had been hastily built in remote parts of the country to house over one hundred thousand Japanese Americans removed from the Pacific

Coast. It was a city unto itself, made up of 42 city blocks and over 500 barracks, which would eventually house 10,000 prisoners. Barbed-wire fences surrounded the settlement, and watchtowers manned by armed guards ensured that no one could escape.

Actually, there was no place to escape *to*. For miles around, there were no cities or towns, no houses—not even any trees. The landscape was totally flat, dotted here and there by a lonely sagebrush. A carpet of ankle-deep sand covered the dry ground.

In this desolate setting the wind howled constantly, carrying with it the gritty white sand that stung people's faces, and often made it impossible to see for all its swirling. Summers were scorchingly hot. Winters were bitterly cold. It was painfully obvious why so few people lived in the region.

The Korematsus were assigned to Block 26, Barrack 9, in which they were allotted two rooms. Each room was lit by a bare light bulb that hung limply from a cord in the ceiling. Except for six metal cots and six Army blankets, the rooms were empty when the Korematsus arrived. If they wanted chairs, tables, or dressers, prisoners had to build them themselves, using

whatever pieces of scrap wood they could find around the camp.

Two rooms to house six adults—at Topaz, like Tanforan, privacy and peace and quiet were nonexistent. It was impossible for the Korematsus to stay out of each other's way in such tight quarters. Even worse, the shoddily built walls meant that everybody knew everyone else's business. Day and night the sounds of talking, crying, laughing, and yelling pierced the thin walls of the barracks.

Every morning at 7 A.M., a siren blast jolted the inmates of Topaz awake. Fred would get up and walk over to his block's mess hall, where he ate all his meals. In the large mess halls, everyone ate at long tables. Parents sat with parents, and children sat with their friends. Fred usually ate by himself.

After breakfast the children went to school. Like children all across America, they began each school day by reciting the Pledge of Allegiance. Hands over their hearts, they pledged their allegiance to "one Nation indivisible, with liberty and justice for all." Then they sang, "My country, 'tis of thee, sweet land of liberty, of thee I sing." Unlike other American school children, however, these children were going to school in large prisons.

Many adults went to work after breakfast. Fred's father worked as part of a six-man crew that helped keep the makeshift dirt roads of the camp in order. Fred dug ditches and helped build the camp hospital. Other inmates worked in the mess halls, camp hospital and office, and store. The inmates' work helped keep the camp running. But the wages Fred and other inmates received for their work were pitiful. The government paid them between $12 and $19 a month. Fred had made $8.50 a day as a free citizen.

The inmates at Topaz did everything they could to lead normal lives in their prison camp. Outside their drab barracks, some people created elegant rock gardens framed by tiny bonsai trees. Others painted watercolors of their surroundings or wrote poetry. Fred's mother made flower arrangements and carved sculptures from cast-off pieces of wood.

Yet, the inmates could never forget that they were living in a heavily guarded prison. An incident that occurred one afternoon in April 1943 was a particularly strong reminder. That day, an elderly Issei man went on a walk around the camp. Wanting to get as close to freedom as he could, he strolled up to the fence that enclosed the camp. Suddenly, a shot rang out, and the man fell to the ground, dead. A guard had fired to kill because he thought the man was trying to escape.

Inmates at Topaz were outraged. Hundreds attended the man's funeral to protest his unjust death. Relations between government staff workers and inmates remained strained for months after.

Another incident reminded inmates of the intensely hostile feelings towards Japanese Americans that existed in the "outside world." In September 1943, a gang of white boys in a car sped past Topaz three times, throwing rocks and spraying gunfire into the community hall. Three inmates were wounded. The boys were caught and put in jail.

In this environment it was easy for Fred to forget about his court case. It didn't seem to matter anymore. Yes, Japanese Americans had been evacuated unjustly. But nothing could be done about that now, just as nothing could be done for the Issei man who had been shot down. The dreams and hopes of the inmates at Topaz seemed lost forever.

For over a year Fred heard nothing about the fate of his case. Then, in December 1943, he received a letter from Ernest Besig. Besig informed Fred that he had lost his case in the Court of Appeals. However, the ACLU was planning to take Fred's case to the highest court in the country, the Supreme Court.

At about this time, Fred was preparing to leave Topaz. The country was in desperate need of more laborers for the war effort, and the government had begun to allow Nisei out of the camps so that they could work. Nisei were also being allowed to attend colleges and universities—as long as they stayed away from the West Coast, and as long as members of the white community would sponsor them. Elderly Issei like Fred's parents, however, were still considered "dangerous aliens" by the government. They were forbidden to go anywhere.

Fred's brother Harry left Topaz to take a job with the state department of agriculture in Utah. His other brothers, Hi and Joe, went to work on a vegetable farm with about twenty other young men from camp. The pay was low and the work was hard, but it was worth it to feel free once again.

Through the camp newspaper, Fred found a job as a welder in Salt Lake City, 140 miles north of Topaz. Being released, however, involved a great deal of red tape. Fred had to fill out many forms. His background and his new bosses were checked and double-checked. Then Fred was asked to swear his unqualified allegiance to the United States and to swear his willingness to defend the country faithfully from all foreign powers. Once that was done, he was approved for release and given still more typewritten forms to fill out after he settled in Salt Lake City.

On the day he left Topaz, Fred was given some pocket money and a booklet called "When You Leave the Relocation Center," which gave advice on how to get along in the "outside world" without offending white Americans. Then he said goodbye to his parents, who were all alone now in the once-crowded rooms of Block 26, Barrack 9.

Fred clambered aboard a truck filled with other Nisei who were headed for Salt Lake City. The truck rumbled up to the camp's main gate and was waved through by the military guard on duty.

For a few minutes, Fred watched the familiar watchtowers and barracks of Topaz grow smaller and smaller behind the clouds of dust kicked up by the truck. Then he turned to watch the horizon unfold in front of him. At last, after having lived behind barbed wire for over a year, Fred was a free man.

10

FREED, BUT NOT CLEARED

At first it was exciting to be in Salt Lake City. Fred eagerly took in the splendor of the majestic, snow-covered mountains around him. It had been a long time since he had seen anything so beautiful. Other sights filled him with a different kind of joy: paved roads, green lawns, one-family homes, corner drugstores. Such luxuries were nonexistent in Topaz. It was hard for Fred to believe that he had once taken these things for granted.

Yet, Salt Lake City was by no means a paradise. Discrimination was as much a part of life there as in California. Fred and his friends lived in one of the only boarding houses that would rent rooms to Japanese Americans. They ate all their meals at the few restaurants that were owned by Nisei. No other restaurants would serve them.

Fred worked at an ironworks, repairing water tanks. But after he had been on the job for three months, he discovered that he and his friends were being paid only half what their white co-workers were being paid. Fred told his boss that this was unfair and asked to be paid the same amount. His boss refused, then threatened to send Fred and his friends back to Topaz. Fred angrily quit the job.

Before long, Fred managed to find another position, but it was dull work, capping car tires. Determined to make more of his life, Fred decided to move east. He had heard that there were many welding jobs available in Detroit, Michigan, and his younger brother Joe was already living and working there.

In Detroit, Fred quickly found a job as a welder. Then Fred's boss discovered that he could draw well, so Fred was promoted to draftsman in one of the company's engineering projects.

Slowly, the future was beginning to look hopeful again to Fred. He even found some romance.

After his devastating breakup with Ida, it was hard for Fred to even think of opening his heart to anyone again. But one night, not long after he had arrived in Detroit, Fred met a young woman at a YMCA dance. Her name was Kathryn Pearson. She had grown up in South Carolina, but now was working as a bacteriologist in a Detroit hospital. The two young Americans began to fall in love.

Then, in December 1944, Fred received a letter from Ernest Besig in San Francisco. It reported that Fred had lost his case before the Supreme Court.

Fred stared at Besig's message in disbelief, feeling a disappointment that was almost beyond words. Fred truly had believed that he would win his case, that the Supreme Court justices would recognize how wrong the evacuation had been.

But the Supreme Court had ruled that the order to evacuate Japanese Americans had been legal. Evacuation represented a valid use of war powers, the justices in the majority ruled, because Japanese Americans appeared at the time to pose a real military threat to American security.

Three justices had dissented from the majority opinion. Justice Owen Roberts wrote, "I need hardly labor the conclusion that constitutional rights have been violated." Justices Robert Jackson and Frank Murphy wrote that the claim that Japanese Americans represented a military threat was not supported by hard evidence. Justice Murphy called the whole evacuation process a "legalization of racism."

Fred's disappointment flared into anger. How could the Supreme Court uphold such a racist action? He tore up Ernest Besig's letter and threw the pieces aside.

That was it, he thought grimly. He had fought for what was right, and he had lost. There was no other authority to which he could appeal. The Supreme Court's unfavorable ruling had put an end to his two-year battle to find justice in the United States of America.

For his own sake, Fred became determined to forget the whole thing. His faith in American justice had been shaken to its very roots, but what choice did he have but to go on? As a result of Executive Order 9066, he was prohibited from going to the West Coast; his parents remained imprisoned at Topaz, their home occupied by strangers; and his brothers were scattered across the country. Unfair as all of this was, what choice did any of them have but to go on?

About the same time that Fred learned of his defeat before the Supreme Court, the government announced that it would close Topaz and other internment camps by the end of 1945. The tide of war had clearly shifted in favor of the United States and its allies by the end of 1944, and it seemed likely that World War II would end during the next year. Military officials were no longer concerned about the perceived threat of Japanese Americans to the West Coast.

Issei who expressed their loyalty to the United States were gradually allowed to return to the West Coast. Many chose to remain in the camps until they officially closed, however. The Issei, after all, had no place to go. Evacuation had stripped them of their homes and businesses, and the elderly men and women had little strength left to start their lives all over again.

Moreover, the West Coast remained fiercely anti-Japanese. Many white farmers were determined to keep their former neighbors from returning and setting up shop again. "We don't want Japs back *EVER*," proclaimed a sign printed by the mayor of the farming community of Kent,

Washington. One farmer printed a full-page newspaper advertisement warning Japanese-American farmers not to return to Hood River, Oregon. "There is published, herewith, the names of about five hundred more Hood River people who do not want you back," he added.

Shots were fired at the homes of returning farmers. Japanese-American produce was boycotted at farmers' markets. In the cities, housing was denied to returning citizens. With little money and nowhere else to go, many Japanese Americans set up makeshift housing in dusty Japanese-language schools, churches, and temples that had been boarded up during the war.

Fred's parents remained at Topaz until it was closed in the fall of 1945. Upon returning to Oakland after their three-and-a-half-year imprisonment, they found their precious nursery in shambles. The gardener who was supposed to have cared for the nursery had made as much money as he could from the Korematsus' roses, but had not maintained the place. Many panes of glass in the greenhouses were broken, and most of the rose bushes had withered and died.

The elderly Korematsus had to start their

once-thriving nursery business all over again. It would take eight years of hard work to bring the business back to the way it had been before they were evacuated.

In the fall of 1946, the Korematsus received an invitation from Fred to attend his wedding in Detroit. He and Kathryn Pearson were getting married. The Korematsus could not make the long journey to Michigan, but they sent a big bouquet of flowers to congratulate their son and his new wife.

After the war ended, Fred concentrated on putting the past behind him and making the most of the rest of his life. He and Kathryn stayed in Detroit for several more years after they were married. Then Fred decided it was time to go back to California. He was ready to return home—to overcome the dark and bitter memories connected with the place and take advantage of all that home had to offer.

Fred and Kathryn settled in San Leandro, not far from the busy corner on which he had been arrested years before. In 1950 Kathryn gave birth to their first child, Karen. Four years later, Kenneth Korematsu was born. Fred continued to work as a draftsman, and in his spare time he played golf and did volunteer work with his church and the local Lions Club.

Until that explosive day in 1967 when Karen listened to her friend Maya's report on Japanese Americans during World War II, neither of Fred's children knew about the prison camps their father had experienced or his courageous stand against them. It seemed that Fred had successfully put the past, with all its humiliation and anger, behind him.

Yet the story of the past was not yet over. For many years it appeared that Fred's case had ended as a true tragedy in 1944. Justice had been denied, never to be restored again. But almost four decades later, in 1982, Fred Korematsu would help forge a new ending to his story.

11

VICTORY AT LAST

On a cold January morning in 1982, Fred Korematsu received a telephone call from a law professor named Peter Irons. Irons said he wanted to show Fred some new documents he had uncovered that related to Fred's 1942 court case.

Forty long years had passed since Fred first went to court over the evacuation of Japanese Americans. He had recently retired from work and was enjoying the first peace and quiet he had ever had in his life. The turmoil of World War II seemed so distant, so safely buried in the past. Yet try as he might, Fred had never been able to put it all fully behind him—the injustice, the hurt, and the anger of that time.

It was rare for Fred to speak with any stranger about his past, but cautiously, he agreed to meet with the law professor. That evening, Irons visited Fred at his home in San Leandro. He handed Fred the documents he had discovered.

The papers were memos written by United States government attorneys in 1943 and 1944. The lawyers had protested that their bosses were hiding evidence that would help Fred's Supreme Court case. Fred studied the documents. He could hardly believe what he was reading.

Back in 1942, Army generals had insisted that Japanese Americans be put in internment camps because they were likely to be disloyal to the United States and therefore posed a military threat. But the papers Fred was now reading said that government lawyers had actually been told to lie to support the generals' claims.

The documents showed that in the fall of 1941—four months before the Japanese attack on Pearl Harbor—a Chicago businessman named Curtis Munson had been asked by President Roosevelt to secretly investigate whether Japanese Americans posed a threat to the United States. Munson later wrote a detailed report to the President telling him there was no need to fear America's Japanese population.

"There will be no armed uprising of Japanese (Americans)," Munson wrote. "For the most part the local Japanese are loyal to the United States or, at worst, hope that by remaining quiet they can avoid concentration camps or irresponsible mobs. We do not believe that they would be at least any more disloyal than any other racial group in the United States with whom we went to war," Munson concluded.

Yet another piece of evidence lay in the pile of documents presented to Fred by Peter Irons. A few days before President Roosevelt signed Executive Order 9066, Attorney General Francis Biddle wrote to the President to express his opposition to Japanese-American evacuation.

"My last advice from the War Department is that there is no evidence of imminent attack and from the FBI that there is no evidence of planned sabotage," Biddle told the President.

The importance of these documents was at once clear to Fred. Had the government lawyers informed the Supreme Court of all the evidence they had at their disposal, he probably would have won his case. But the government lawyers had hidden key information from the Supreme Court justices.

"They did me a great wrong," Fred said at last,

raising his eyes from the documents. He looked at Peter Irons. After forty years of silence, Fred was ready to challenge the government again.

"Are you a lawyer?" he asked Irons.

"Yes, I am," Irons said.

"Would you be my lawyer?" Fred asked.

"I'd be delighted," Irons said without hesitation.

There was much research to be done. First, Irons hired a young lawyer named Dale Minami to help with the case. Then the two lawyers and many dedicated volunteers spent well over a year preparing for the trial. Finally, on November 10, 1983, Fred appeared in federal court in San Francisco.

A crowd of three hundred people crammed into the courtroom. Many of the spectators were elderly Japanese Americans who, like Fred and his family, had been imprisoned in internment camps. They came to give Fred moral support. An air of expectancy filled the crowded room.

The trial began with a request by government lawyers to stop the hearing. Judge Marilyn Patel rejected their request. Then Dale Minami rose from his seat and began his argument in defense of Fred. The courtroom was still.

"We are here today to seek a measure of justice denied to Fred Korematsu and the Japanese-American community forty years ago," Minami began forcefully.

He went on to argue that Fred had lost his case in 1944 because the lawyers for the government had lied and concealed important information. Had they presented that information to the Supreme Court, Minami stressed, it would have proven that there was no evidence showing that Japanese Americans posed a threat to the United States.

Minami explained that Fred had fought the case by himself because other Japanese Americans had been too frightened to fight. "For the Japanese-American community, Fred's fight was their fight," the lawyer said. Then he emphasized, "this is the last opportunity to finally achieve the justice denied forty years ago."

When he was finished speaking, Dale Minami asked Judge Patel if Fred could address the court. Judge Patel agreed.

Fred rose from his chair. He spoke softly before the hushed courtroom. "Your Honor," he began, "I still remember forty years ago when I was handcuffed and arrested as a criminal here in San Francisco." Then he described the suffer-

ing that he and his family, and all Japanese Americans, had endured in the camps.

"As long as my record stands in federal court, any American citizen can be held in prison or concentration camps without a trial or a hearing," Fred said. Then he made a simple request: "I would like to see the government admit that they were wrong and do something about it so this will never happen again to any American citizen of any race, creed, or color."

After Fred spoke, a government lawyer made a brief statement. The courtroom buzzed when the lawyer had finished. The new evidence Fred had brought forth had indeed made a strong case. After so many years, would justice finally be done?

All attention was focused on Judge Patel as she prepared to make her ruling. Fred held his breath, waiting for the judge's words.

Judge Patel ruled in Fred's favor. Once the meaning of her ruling became clear, the courtroom erupted with cheering and clapping.

Fred was overjoyed. At long last, he had won his case against the United States government. He had finally succeeded in getting a fair trial.

Fred, who had fought his case all alone forty years earlier, was now surrounded by Japanese Americans of all ages wanting to congratulate him. Many cried tears of joy. It was a bittersweet end to a long nightmare. While nothing could restore all that had been taken away from the Japanese Americans who had been imprisoned, the government's admission of wrongdoing at least restored honor to those imprisoned. And, it offered the hope that a similar act of tyranny would never again happen in the United States.

On the day of his victory, Fred's daughter Karen, now 33 years old, was out of the country on a business trip. But that night she called home to find out the verdict. Her mother told her the wonderful news.

Karen was thrilled. She remembered only too well what it had been like to be one of the only two Japanese Americans in class. She remembered, too, how painful it had been for her father to talk about his experiences during World War II.

Karen was proud of her father for having had the courage to continue his fight despite all the injustice he had endured. Most of all, she was proud of him for what he had done for the

Japanese-American community, and indeed for all Americans. By fighting for his rights, Fred Toyosaburo Korematsu had worked to protect the rights of every American to "liberty and justice for all."

Afterword

The story told here is true. *When Justice Failed* is based primarily on Fred Korematsu's memories of his life and times. Other interviews and a number of written accounts of the internment were extremely helpful in rounding out Fred's story. Some ordinary details—clear blue skies yawning overhead, children riding bicycles, dust swirling around the wheels of a truck—are made up. But nothing of importance has been changed or added. All the dialogue that appears within quotation marks consists of the actual words that were written down and recorded at the time or are the words that Fred remembers as being spoken.

We would like to thank Fred Korematsu and his family for their cooperation in the writing of this book. Special thanks are also extended to Ruth Akamine and Steve Stern for their able assistance in the final preparation of this story.

Notes

Pages 1–3 The United States entered World War II on December 8, 1941, the day after Japanese warplanes attacked an American naval base at Pearl Harbor, Hawaii. The base was caught totally off-guard, and more than two thousand Americans were killed. Japan's prime minister at the time, Hideki Tojo, quickly became as much of a hated villain in the eyes of Americans as the dictator of Germany, Adolf Hitler.

Pages 5–9 Ken Korematsu, Karen's younger brother, was to experience the same painful and confusing revelation that Karen had experienced in Mr. Wishnoff's class. Several years later, in one of his social studies classes, Ken too learned of his father's defiant stand against the government's imprisonment of Japanese Americans.

Pages 11–12 Fred's father, Kakusaburo Korematsu, opened his nursery in the early 1900s. At that time it was hard for Japanese immigrants like himself to succeed in America. Asian immigrants were viewed as a threat to white laborers in the west, just as immigrants from southern and eastern Europe were considered threats to workers in the eastern United States.

Around western cities and towns it was not uncommon to see signs and graffiti scrawled: "Fire the Japs!" and "Japs Go Away!" White Americans usually refused to hire Japanese people for jobs unless they needed farm laborers, gardeners, or house servants—jobs considered undesirable by most white people. Laws prevented the Japanese immigrants from owning land or gaining American citizenship.

Through it all, however, Japanese immigrants persevered. They worked hard and saved all the money they could. They skirted the unfair land laws by buying land in the names of their American-born children or paying white people to buy land for them. Yet these tactics were not foolproof, and the Japanese immigrants lived in constant fear of being found out by the government or being betrayed by the people to whom they had entrusted their land titles.

Page 11 Fred and his family lived in the southern section of Oakland, close to the town of San Leandro.

Pages 20–21 Not long after he was turned down at the recruitment office, Fred was required by law to appear before a draft board. Congress had begun the process of drafting men into the armed services. This time Fred was rejected on medical grounds because he reportedly had ulcers.

Pages 21–24 Anti-Japanese sentiment was deeply ingrained in Fred's union. After the bombing of Pearl Harbor, the union actually expelled all Japanese-American members from its ranks. The Boilermakers' Union was by no means the only group to take such racist actions.

Pages 29–30 By December 10, just three days after Pearl Harbor, the FBI had arrested more than 1,200 Japanese-American citizens and was holding them for questioning. Meanwhile, the Army was reporting a steady stream of terrifying news: Japanese bombers are approaching San Francisco! Japanese warships are heading for the California coast! Los Angeles is about to be attacked! All these reports proved to be unfounded. So, too, were the fears that Japanese Americans were agents of the Japanese government. The FBI informed President Roosevelt that it had found no suspicious evidence in the hands of Japanese Americans. Its findings, however, were covered up.

Pages 32–34 The idea of "removing" Japanese Americans was not a new one. Five years before the attack on Pearl Harbor, President Franklin Roosevelt himself was already privately considering ways to put

Japanese Americans "in a concentration camp in the event of trouble." In 1939 an American Legion leader proclaimed, "In the case of war, the first thing I would do would be to intern every one of" the Japanese Americans.

Much was at stake in removal. Japanese Americans had converted unproductive, unwanted lands into rich, productive farms worth millions of dollars. One white farm leader admitted, "We're charged with wanting to get rid of the Japs for selfish reasons. We might as well be honest. We do. It's a question of whether the white man lives on the Pacific Coast or the brown men."

Page 34 Lieutenant General De Witt was hardly alone in his opinions. California's attorney general and soon-to-be governor, Earl Warren, believed that there were ways to test the loyalty of German and Italian Americans. But "when we deal with the Japanese," he claimed, "we are in an entirely different field." Warren was convinced that the total lack of evidence against Japanese Americans was the greatest proof of all that they were planning something terrible. No evidence was suddenly evidence! Ironically, Earl Warren would go on to become one of the most humanitarian justices of the United States Supreme Court, and in December 1983, Fred Korematsu would receive the prestigious Earl Warren Human Rights Award from the ACLU.

Page 40 Many Japanese-American families were not as fortunate as the Korematsus and had to sell all their belongings before being evacuated. White

Americans bargained coldly with these desperate families. They offered five or ten dollars for refrigerators and washing machines, a mere fraction of the goods' actual worth. The owners had no choice but to accept the ridiculous low offers.

Page 56 Tanforan was one of seventeen assembly centers operated by the Army in California, Oregon, Washington, and Arizona. Several of the centers were converted race tracks, fairgrounds, and livestock exhibition halls. In Washington, newspapers reassured an indignant public that Japanese Americans imprisoned at the fairgrounds in Puyallup would be removed in time for the annual state fair.

Pages 71–72 Topaz was one of ten camps built to house Japanese-American prisoners. Manzanar and Tule Lake were built in California. Poston and Gila were constructed in Arizona. Heart Mountain was built in Wyoming, Minidoka in Idaho, and Granada in Colorado. The two camps farthest from the West Coast, Jerome and Rohwer, were located in Arkansas.

Pages 75–76 Relations between government staff workers and inmates were already strained by a questionnaire that the government required all prisoners to fill out. The questionnaire centered around two questions. The first asked whether the person was willing to serve in the United States armed forces in combat duty. The second asked if the person would swear "unqualified allegiance" to the United States and "forswear any form of allegiance or obedience to the Japanese emperor, or any other foreign government."

Many prisoners were enraged by these questions. Nisei bitterly resented being forced to swear allegiance to the very country that was betraying them and stripping them of their rights as citizens. Issei found themselves in a no-win situation. They were barred by law from becoming American citizens to begin with. Now they were being called upon to renounce the only citizenship they were permitted, that of Japan. To do so would leave them a people without a country.

Almost nine thousand people—mostly Nisei— responded no to both questions. They were branded "disloyal" by the government and shipped off to the Tule Lake camp, which in the summer of 1943 was transformed into a high-security prison renamed the Tule Lake Segregation Center. Six tanks and over one thousand soldiers patrolled the facility. Angry and embittered prisoners lashed out through riots and strikes against the government that was oppressing them. Martial law was imposed.

By 1945, many of the Nisei at Tule Lake had become so disillusioned with the United States that they renounced their American citizenship. In November 1945, over fifteen hundred people said goodbye to their families and friends and boarded ships headed for Japan—the Japan so recently leveled by American atomic bombs and other weapons of destruction. Many had never before been to Japan.

Page 89 Beginning in the late 1960s, children of former prisoners began speaking out against what had happened to their parents. Together with their parents and other allies, they began to press the government to admit that what it had done to Japanese Americans during World War II was wrong. The "redress" movement gained its greatest momentum during the early 1980s, at about the time that Professor Irons was contacting Fred Korematsu.

Page 92 Dale Minami had an especially personal interest in Fred's case. His parents had been imprisoned in the Heart Mountain camp in Wyoming.

Page 96 In 1988 Congress passed a bill that apologized to Japanese Americans and provided a payment of twenty thousand dollars to each individual still living who had been imprisoned. The actions of Congress came too late for many Issei like Fred's parents, who had died long before the passage of the bill. The money also failed to adequately compensate Japanese Americans for all that they had lost because of Executive Order 9066. However, the bill did help to restore the honor of those who had been wrongfully imprisoned during World War II. It also helped reaffirm the country's commitment to the principle of justice.

Steven A. Chin is a newspaper reporter for the *San Francisco Examiner*. He received the Outstanding Young Journalist Award for his newspaper reporting in 1991. Mr. Chin also wrote *Dragon Parade*.